T0063335

No Missions for Masters

The Peking Order and other Poems and Short Stories

ARMEN A. DOVLETIAN

Order this book online at www.trafford.com
or email orders@trafford.com

Most Trafford titles are also available at major online book retailers.

Printed in the United States of America.

ISBN: 978-1-4907-4235-9 (sc)
ISBN: 978-1-4907-4236-6 (e)

Library of Congress Control Number: 2014913018

Trafford rev. 09/04/2014

Trafford
PUBLISHING®   www.trafford.com
North America & international
toll-free: 1 888 232 4444 (USA & Canada)
fax: 812 355 4082

– A collection of poetry
and short stories..

– College educated working –
class hero puts
pen to paper..
A few surprises!

To whom it may concern

Peking Order Man was the most evolved hominoid for his brain size for his time.

The Peking Order was a secret band of martial artists in China who set out to save the world from a powerful dictator around the turn of the century.

"Jeesh," said Mark, "It's getting hot." I said it was.. and was alot.
"May I have," asked John, "A glass of juice?" Kevin just laughed,, and said, "It's no use."
"We can take showers," I responded, "In turns, of course."
Wayne said, "Hurry please,, I'm getting hoarse,"

'That's odd,' she thought,, as she read the note,, 'what did he mean by 'Take the boat'?'

Dear Tick:

Please go away.

1

I guess I did that..
Put pennies back-to-back..
Had the thought, 'Electric crack..'
And boy and girl were set free..
Had the thought, 'so do we,'

"I think that today I will cook clean and noman."

"What is noman?"

"No man is an island."

My Dear Wormwood:

As for that pork loin that was left over the other night when we had that terrible row..
Eat it now and all will be forgiven..

Your loving uncle..

Screwtape

A Hundred Generations Square
The Almighty Orange..
Must he lay fallow to?

"I killed my brother in Washington."
So Spokane

"Y-e-e-s-s!" she laughed
"Sell us the pot and come over
for supper!"

The West River

When you go to France
Don't forget to take in
the Paris sights.

And then was the Hunting
And the moths would come out..
to get clapped on their ears,
And dropped with a shout.

Your very perspective.

In the brush
In the briar
Roughly shod
Higher higher
Spill the blood
Turn to mire
Bless this world
Of bolt and tire!
Would it could be otherwise!
Oh, perhaps to change the guise!
Go your way, peaceably
And love for you
will always be.

Because it was mete.

The Greening of the Pampas.

If the time were truly
7:70 on the dot..
It would soon be found out
If some liked it hot..
For Martin had proved
time and again
that he couldn't show up
at the appointed when!
And.. Like it or not..
Despite almost a tot..
He could find himself back
back on the Aeroflot!
How he had cried
to come to this land!
Had he not a right
to the soda and sand?
But judgement was against him
down to a man..
to give him the much
well deserved can.

Not writing distrighting
Not writing its frighting.
Not writing distrighting
Not writing its frighting!

Woods explode in sunshine green
Everything's more than it would seem.

Not writing
You're not writing
I'm encreiting
worse yet,,
It's distrighting.

The Life of a man

Foxen shadows

Pictures of nowhere
And livid green lines
Bedecked cedar barrels
that held only wine.

My poor sick seagull mated
for life as could be expected
he took a tern for the worse.

Thinking, thinking
getting deeper..
Teapot's sitting
Getting steeper.

Friends I have none..
but the ones I have some.

And so it was said.. And repeated twice.. that you shall not eat meat with your fingers rice.. step on a fork or write nonsense wice.. For handed down from grandma to pop was the decree that you shall not stop to kiss the flowers or throw the stones nor believe in such things as Dolly clones.

I suppose
It grows in Rose
around your toes
Like sucrolose

Don't say but
when you're in a rut
your queesy gut
You crazy nut

My those people have a way
of weaving through crowds
with a swish swash sway.
I've marked them in my
          mind of mine.,
especially at times when its
appropriate to dine..
If approached and demanded
to speak..
I would aknowledge there
          was a leak
Of information about the union.

There was a robbery at the Toy Store..
Raggedy Ann was called in as a
          material witness.

How crass the grass
where lass did pass,,
"A mass," quote Tass
"For small mouth bass."

When crossing your legs
          Remember:
Right over left is the
Left over right.

To dance perchance and
            so enhance
the trance of Lance performed
          in France.

Somebody get the catti out of
          the tranni!

See the farmbirds on the fence..
See them crap on boyscout tents..

Cowboys cowboys everywhere
try to get a breath of air

Now its time for me to up
Pass me please my coffee cup

As I even out the odds of gamble
And make my way to work preamble.

Wasn't it Arjuna who said..
"It's not the T.V.
it's the transmission.."

"You're going to need a shoot," he said..
"I have one," I said.. and jumped out of the plane.

The hedgehog in the hedgerow cries
to have some ketchup on his fries
As giraffes pace the floors at home
And wonder who will patch the dome.

I have a peculiar habit
The one described so well in Babbit
Of murdering little varmints
While clad only in my under garments.

"Ape rill" said the biologist decidedly
And ran his fingers
          through the muck and undergrowth

To be a subject of the Terrible One..
And the Infinite One.. Mars.

Zero was a play soldier.

Familiarity breeds contempt..
Abcess makes the heart grow fondue.

I've seen them once
I've see them twice
They stand in corners
with palms of rice
A peck a day
What do in hay?
And still they turn
The spool of Pern.

Left right
In the middle

Always wear their knot..
Always where they're not.

Roan stallone with your bit of brass.
You pull your load of blood and carnage.
For a krugerand or less for your keeper Seth..
He'd slit your bonds in minutes flat
You'd walk the streets with a yellow hat
A bag of mixed flours
says there's going to be a fish fry today,,
The kids will cry cry
but they'll get a piece..
And you'll get one, too!

Patches of blue
So are you
In my pants
Raves and rants

Circle of mud
Oh what crud
Paint the house
Without a blouse

Stiller times
I have known
Oh! What rhymes with maid and blown!

Kiss your shoes
Oh what's the use!
You'll just have me
If I'm loose.

Bridge under the water
where the aligators were..
I saw something move but continued to stir
No mention made
of that sunny glade
Nor the way we enjoyed ourselves on the day it was made.
That was 5,000 yrs.
Though I break into tears
I tell the folk that t'was really no joke.

Man is born in pain
And spends his life in chains.

"Armen!.. Armen are you there?
Armen.. where are you?"
"Half by the phone half I'm alone..
          wait but a moment and you'll hear a tone.."
"Then go yea with your phone
and tone.. A half a moment?
The times well sown!"
"Much will we have to talk about.,
About how that lout did all but shout.."
"And how the one on the other end
was really truly a best friend."

Einfach kommen die Manner zu..
Haben nicht und nicht zu tu'.

"We Lost the War!"

- General Lee
speaking

Hordes of natives running
across a plain yelling,
"MEAT MEAT"

Ice on snow on snow on ice.

Check the dishwasher
See if the meatloaf is ready.

Bagavad Gita on chimney top,,
the birds,, the green would not to stop.

Swept by their crying
the beatles have found
their insides their words
have made clean all around.

"Mom,, what's the flooding for?"

Not really employed..
Generally irresponsible.

As dice were tossed and fortunes broke
The sun came up.. I took a toke.
"Looks like rain," I said to me..
"Pardon me, sir," I said, "but do you have a bee?"
I looked that man.. of glassine fish..
And wondered how he could be dished.
I punched him once,, I punched him twice
7 yrs. bad luck,, it serves him right
No time for pun.. the proof is writ!
I broke my pen forgot to spit!
Just as I'd have another score
the Judge yelled out, "For you no more!"

I'm in a prison of my own making."

"You didn't make this!"

"O.K.! So I lie sometimes!"

The grew of pot of Milton Dew
was all the townfolk of Doc Henerson knew
And if they thought his first name Lou
they were in for a treat,, one or two.
And "why?" they asked,, when they later found out
was answered and whet with string of doubt
The response was sharp and delivered
with clout.. Kilarjin did his job and that he did tout
"My" said Bob, "This is not my game,, The game of playing
games with your name."
"Aye," said I, "know its much the same,"
"And father chimed in, "It's about a dame!"
There was no one left in that small town.. when the 3 or 4
of them walked round watership down..
The rabbit on the moon and Irish coin was what they knew
they were destined to join.

Beluze beluze beluze gauze
That was the reason,, that was the cause
We had our ways, we had our laws
but in the long run the winner was beluze gauze
And writ in the middle
        of books of the same
were many to many significant name
It wasn't a hobby it wasn't a game
Just more or less more or less of the same.

I suppose that Tibet is a
troublesome province of China?

"Of course," I cried, "And would again!"
And saying this I closed my pen.
Refusing to rate can lose your place
A worser fate than fall from grace,,
I'd tried the vendors with not much luck,,
A piece of chicken and some Cold Duck,,
for an evening snack is had by many
who care to part with a pretty penny.
Wandering about the streets of my new town
As I was wont to in my evening gown
I've had the chance to talk to some,,
who stop in that shop to purchase rum
But over and over I tell myself
to ignore that sign requesting "HELF".

"Do you know what time is?" The man asked pointing to my watch.

"That's pretty heavy," I said. "So is this," the man said,, and proceeded to haul it out of my office on his back.

As the world goes spinning round
We find we're waiting for Gabriel's sound
As we pour coffee on the ground
And get together to dig a mound.
There, no doubt, it can be found
The bones of the Baskerville hound
And due respects may abound
If meted out pound by pound
From the axis from which they're wound.

Leader: To score some more and still adore
Chorus: That is what a wife is for

L   The birds and bees they have their way
C   And you'll have yours sometime today

L   If times an issue check the clock
C   You're a chip off the old block

L   We sometimes need to be alone
C   Consider well the plant and stone

L   She covers us, we cover her
C   That's what makes the Lion purr.

"Mommy.. what's an alcoholic?"

"I know your kind.."
"I know you're generous.."

Only in Mexico

The crow was flying over the green mountains his black body in the sun casting a shadow on the brush below,,
Of a sudden the shadow flew off leaving the crow in the air!

To fight! Tonight! Over Dover right!
We'll hop a fence and jump a train..
We'll drink some beer and clean the drain..
I think it fair.. that we should pare..
some apples each.. for English teach..
And switch the poles, of motor's charge..
So as to see,, that band at large.

Footprints

I was retracing my footprints in the sand with God one day.

Of a sudden I noticed but one set of footprints... I became troubled.. "My God, my God," I cried out, "Why did you forsake me?" My Father said, "My son, my son,, I love you very much I would never leave you.. where you saw one set of footprints that was when I carried you."

There was a note.. and it was
a t o n e

Armen Dovletian

I'm an old veteran
Near old Vietnam
NV elan mediator
Am in ND elevator
Mr. Valentine DOA
Revel damnation
Nova derailment
Am in NEA Devo LTR